Contents

1 Skateboarding

Skateboarding is for everyone.
You don't need much money.
You can do it on the streets, in the park,
in a back yard or at a skate park.
You can do it on your own
or with your friends.

You can learn the basics and have fun
but if you keep going
there is always something new to learn.
That's what is so good.
There is always a new trick to learn.

It's fast.
The record speed for lying flat on a board
going downhill is 70 mph.
A good speed is 30 mph.
That's fast when it's just you and a board.

You need good balance.

Do you want to try?
You need to be fit or get fit
as it's hard work.
You need good balance
but you'll get better with practice.

To be good, your mind and body
need to be as one.
Relax, keep your mind on what you are doing
and you succeed.
When fear gets in the way
or you think of something else, you fall.

Can you deal with pain?
There is quite a lot of that.
Can you deal with fear?
It's scary trying something new
and if you fall it can hurt.
When you are scared and tense
a fall hurts and you can break a bone.
If you are relaxed,
you get away with what you shouldn't.

It's about setting yourself a target,
and then sticking to it.
The good thing is
that you set your own targets.
Each step makes you feel good,
because you have to work at it.

Standing up on a board is hard,
the first trick is hard
and it doesn't get easier.
Getting better is doing something
that was impossible yesterday.

You need to keep practising.

2 What Do You Need?

All you need is a skateboard.
First there is the board.
Then there are the trucks
which screw into the board
and hold the wheels.
Bolts screw the trucks to the board.
Then there are the wheels
and the wheel bearings.
Griptape goes on top of the board.

You buy the bits separately
and put your board together.
A skateboard can cost up to £130
or you can buy one second hand.

Shops sell boards for around £20 or £30.
These are OK to start with
but they are not much good for tricks.

You need good shoes that grip,
such as trainers.
Be warned – they can wear out quickly!
Some people wear helmets
and knee pads to protect themselves.

Make sure you are well protected – falls can hurt!

3 Tricks

Tricks are what skateboarding is all about.
Watch a good skateboarder and it's magic.
Body and board twist and fly through the air.

An Ollie

This is the basic trick
for moving along the flat ground.
You and the board jump
and leave the ground.
You have to learn how to jump.
Push down on the back of the board
with your back foot.
The four wheels leave the ground
and the board stands up.
Then drag your other foot up the board
so it goes flat and is off the ground.
Then down comes the board –
and that's an ollie.

A Kickflip

Start with an ollie
but this time the front foot
turns the board over.

A Popshovit

This trick is all in the back foot.
The board turns round instead of over.

You can put these together
to make difficult tricks.

An ollie.

With some tricks
you don't use the wheels at all.
These are grinding tricks.
You ollie onto a wall
and grind along it on your trucks.
The wheels are on either side.
This is called a 50.50.

You can grind along
just on the back of your truck
with the front in the air.
This is called a 5.0.

There are hundreds of different tricks.
You can never learn them all.

You learn to jump high
and keep off the ground.
This gives you time to play with your board
and do amazing things.

When you are good,
your board becomes part of you.
Then you can use your body to twist and turn
and that is part of the trick too.
The board and you
twisting and turning together.

4 Where to Go?

The Skate Park

Some skateboarders go to a skate park.
It's a place to practise
and check out new tricks.
It is all set up with ramps,
the flat and rails.

There may be a street course
with quarter pipes and a fun box.
With a fun box,
you ride up the ramp, hit the box,
do a trick and ride down the other side.

Skateboarding around the inside of a pipe.

Then there are ramps.
There's a mini ramp
and bigger ramps.
The lip or top of the ramp
lets you do grinding tricks.

A few parks have full pipes.
There's only one in the UK in Manchester.
Only two people in the world
have skated right round
the inside of a pipe.

The Streets

Some people use the streets.
They use boards as a way of getting around.

Skateboarders look at streets
in a different way from others.
They see steps and bumps.
They see how a wall meets the ground,
and how high it is.
The top of the wall is important, too.
Empty bins and empty plant holders
are all something to use.

The tricks you do on the streets
and on the flat are different
from skateboarding in a park.

Most cities have a place
where skateboarders meet and practise.
Ask around and find out where it is.

5 Making Money

If you are really good at something,
you never know what's around the corner.
There are ways of making money
with skateboarding.
This is how some people have done it.

Matt   I'm 21.
I work in a skate park.
I make sure everything is OK.
I open up, take money, stuff like that.
It's fun to skate the park
and get paid for it –
but sometimes I want a change
and go and skate on the streets.

Mark   I am 28.
I'm a professional.
I've been skateboarding for 15 years.
I go in for competitions in England and
abroad.
Sometimes I win.
The most I've won is $10,000 in a year.
The top prize money is about $60,000
for big competitions.

I get different companies to sponsor me
and use their logo on my board and clothes.
The money I get from them helps with
boards and fares.
It's like any sport.
If you are good
you may find a sponsor.

I also do videos for my sponsors.
That's a big part of being a professional.
All the big names do advertising videos
and they want the best skateboarders.

A skateboarding competition in America.

Anna I get to skate in films and ads.
I have to keep up with all the latest tricks.
Sometimes I do pretty dangerous stunts.
I'm lucky because there aren't many women
who skateboard, so there's less competition.

One day I was skating on the streets
where skateboarders hang out.
A man came up
and offered me a try out for an ad.
That's how I started.

I don't make enough to live on
so I also work for a skateboard company
in sales.

Jo I'm 35.
    I've been skating for 20 years, on and off.
    I work for a skateboard magazine.
    I work in a team
    and we put the thing together.
    I write about competitions
    and interview skateboarders.
    It's a great job
    and I get to meet all the best skaters.

Seth I run a skateboard shop.
    I work from ten to six.
    I buy boards, wheels, magazines
    and clothes for the shop.
    I get to see all the new stuff first.

    I love skateboarding
    and it's a great job
    but it's sometimes a drag
    when fun becomes work.

6 Finding Out More

Magazines

Sidewalk Surfer (UK)
Thrasher (US)
Slap (US)
Slam (Australia)

These have pictures of tricks and how to do them.
There are interviews with skateboarders
and news of what's going on.

Videos

A good one to start with is
Basics of Skateboarding,
but there are lots to choose from.

Skateboard Shops

These sell everything you need.
Also the people who work there
know what is going on
and pass on local news and information.

If you don't live near a shop try Mail Order:
Slam City Skates, Neals Yard, London WC2.

Internet

There is plenty to check out.
Search 'Skateboarding' and see what comes up.
The personal pages are fun.

Yahoo have a home page on skateboarding.
This connects to clubs, events, equipment
and personal pages:
http://dir.yahoo.com/Recreation
/Sports/Skateboarding/

The site for Playstation skatepark in London is:
www.roadrunner.co.uk/pssp

7 Glossary of Terms Used

Fun box   A special box used at skate parks. You ride up the ramp, hit the box, do a trick and ride down the other side.

Grinding   Using the trucks instead of the wheels.

Grinding trick A trick using the metal trucks and not the wheels.

Griptape   Tape which goes on top of the board and helps you to grip on.

Kickflip   An ollie trick where the front foot turns the board over.

Ollie   A trick involving a jump on flat ground.

Pipe	A curved surface to skate on, such as the inside of a big pipe. (A quarter pipe is a quarter of a circle, and a full pipe is one with no breaks – you skate right round the inside of the pipe.)
Popshovit	A trick where the board turns round instead of over.
Ramp	A slanting surface to skateboard on.
Sponsor	A company (or person) that gives you money in return for being able to advertise their goods or services on your board and equipment.
Trucks	A long piece of metal which screws into the board and to which the wheels are fixed.
Wheel bearings	These are found inside the wheels and make them spin round.